OUR MISTAKES, OUR PAIN, OUR MINISTRY!

Author
Nicole Y. Bowens

Co-Author
Adrian B. Bowens

Copyright © 2018 by Nicole Y. Bowens

Published by: **Marriages of the Kingdom**
Greenville, South Carolina

Cover Design by Unveiled Creations - Greer, South Carolina

Manuscript Format by Effectual Concepts - Greenville, South Carolina

ISBN: 0692104739
ISBN-13: 978-0692104736

To contact the authors or purchase additional books, visit us at: **www.marriagesofthekingdom.com**

DEDICATION

To our children **Nicolas**, **Corey**, **Kimberly**, **Kirkland** and our grandson **Dallas**. We want you to know that marriage can be beautiful, even though you all have experienced being raised in broken homes, just as we did in the past.

We thank God for allowing us through our "ONENESS" to demonstrate to you what marriage looks like when God is given full control and access to your life.

To those who have experienced divorce, to those who feel their marriage is a losing battle, to those who have never been married and have the desire to have a spouse and to those couples who seek direction because they are willing to put in the work necessary to have a Christ-centered marriage.

We want to encourage each of you to **NEVER GIVE UP!**

CONTENTS

Our Mistakes, Our Pain, Our Ministry!

FOREWORD

In our search for happiness and fulfillment, we often follow our own agenda, which causes us to run ahead of God's plan for our well-being. It's easy to forget that God ordained marriage. His revelation to us begins with marriage, Adam and Eve in the garden of Eden, and will end with the marriage of the lamb.

It is not often that someone would address the pitfalls that we encounter searching for true companionship. We cannot help but be grateful to the Bowens for their efforts. Our prayer is that this work will encourage and strengthen marriages of all who read it. May God bless and enrich their ministry as they go forward.

"Marriage is ordained by God. It is an honorable estate, not to be entered into lightly, but with the knowledge that you've made a sacred vow before the Lord."

Pastor G.W. Dixon and Jessie Dixon
~ 57 years happily married ~

Our Mistakes, Our Pain, Our Ministry!

INTRODUCTION

*On May 27, 2017, I was about to enter words of encouragement in our face book group **Marriages of the Kingdom** and I heard God so clearly speak to me, "put it in a book". It is my prayer and hope that Our Mistakes, Our Pain, Our Ministry blesses your marriage and to those that are single I pray it gives you a foundation to begin a healthy and God-centered marriage!*

May God's Peace Rest Upon You!
Nicole Y. Bowens

Our Mistakes, Our Pain, Our Ministry!

CHAPTER 1

OUR JOURNEY

Journey To My King – A Word From Nicole

As I reflect back over my childhood as a young girl, I remember being in the midst of a lot of family members who were married for many years, however I never remember seeing "love". I came from a broken home, my parents divorced when I was around 2 years old and my father was physically abusive to my mother, which created an altercation in which my brother who was 17 years old at the time, was shot and killed by my father, who was his stepfather.

My mother never re-married, because she never moved past the hurt and pain of losing a child, at this point she somewhat checked out on life. My father re-married some time later which was not a healthy marriage either; he had always been an excellent provider financially, but not necessarily the best husband. He was an amazing dad, but a horrible husband from what I saw growing up, he was also physically abusive to my step-mother. Therefore, I never saw a healthy marriage growing up and I was left to figure life out on my own, which lead to a lot of bad decision making. I had two wonderful sons prior to being married, due to a lack of spiritual guidance and simply attending church with a lack of relationship with God. At this time, I did not feel marriage was necessary, neither was abstinence from sex necessary, because I lacked knowledge of God's Word and His plan for my life.

Some years later, I married a close friend which was a huge mistake this lasted briefly, because we connected through our brokenness and we departed in peace. After some time, *still broken*, I walked into a marriage in which I knew it was not God; this decision created much pain, disappointment and anger. I believe the reason this relationship lasted for the period of time it did, was because I refused to quit even though I knew God was not involved. I knew that marriage was of my own doing, I never consulted with God regarding that decision which created much pain. This relationship I had entered actually caused me to compromise my relationship with God, because it did not begin in a godly manner.

Sometimes we make mistakes and try to cover them up and dress them up, because we don't want to admit it was a mistake from the beginning. In marriage you can't go back once you say "I do" so easily. Looking back I realize I never evaluated my "why" before saying "I do". After numerous years of trying to make an unhealthy marriage work it ended in divorce, primarily due to the fact that we were never equally yoked. I realized after the fact, that I viewed my previous marriage more so as a business relationship as opposed to a marriage.

After making a decision in my mind that I would never re-marry after this. I sat down one day and I asked God to reveal to me myself and who I truly was and He started to download into me the good, bad and the ugly. This is when I realized I was saved through the Blood of Jesus, but not completely obedient to the Word of God as it pertained to marriage and my life in general. I was saved and going to heaven, but woke up one day and realized God had so much more in store for me than that. This is where I began through the Word of God rebuilding myself spiritually and submitted my entire life to God for reconstruction.

Through purging my old self and filling myself through the Word of God and prayer, I began to regain strength spiritually and God's plan for my life became very clear to me. God then started speaking to me about the attributes of a Godly wife, what to say or not to say to your husband and how to build him. Even though I said I would never re-marry, at this point I knew I would at some point, because God would not give me this information and not allow me to utilize it.

At this point, I became very specific with my prayers, I said to God, "if I am to re-marry my husband must be submitted to You, not just going to church but living a life that reflects your Word", I also told God he could not have any young children along with many other requests, I made known. I knew God well enough to know that my requests would be honored through the power of prayer and my obedience to Him, according to His will.

God showed me that it was possible to have a beautiful and lifelong marriage if I would allow Him to direct it.

I thank God for giving me another chance to experience true love His way. God hand molded me and renewed my mind for His glory and for my marriage to my husband Adrian.

Journey To My Queen – A Word From Adrian

As a young boy, I was raised by a single mother; however my upbringing included a whole village of family members. Although I was an only child to my mother, I was raised around a plethora of family members; from grandparents, uncles, aunts, and cousins. I wasn't raised around my father, my parents separated before I was born. Through this I never really observed what marriage would look like from my mother and father, which is what we emulate and imitate as we grow up.

My greatest teaching of what marriage and love is came from the Spirit of God. My connection with the Holy Spirit gave me the ability to hear from Him and view marriage differently.

Even though I wasn't raised with parents in a home of our own, I always knew that someday I would be married. When it comes to marriage, I saw some while growing up but for the most part I saw the single life. Even by seeing this, I knew that someday marriage would be a part of my life.

While my first marriage ended in divorce, it was over years before it was actually finalized. I threw in the towel vowing to never get married again. Going forth, I knew God had been waiting on me to change and get back in the "saddle". Going back to that time of separation and divorce, God began to do a work on me. I prayed and asked God to show me myself and where I went wrong and things I could have

5

done differently. I asked God to help me instead of pointing the finger at others. So, as He showed me myself, He purged me of wrong thinking and wrong actions.

Even as God showed me my mistakes, He began to build me up again and make me strong. He started telling me that I was made for marriage. After going through a divorce, I had made up my mind that marriage was not for me and I remember saying several times I would never get married again. Little did I know at this time, that not only would I get married again, but it actually happened that very same year.

The *journey* to get to us was well worth it! There is always glory on the other side of your valley experience! On October 8, 2011, our wedding date, we stepped into our purpose!

Our marriage flourishes now, because of our OBEDIENCE to God's direction!!

Just as God covers and protects us, He placed the husband over the wife; not to dominate her, but to protect her and give her a sense of stability and peace within the marriage. Women, submission does not make you weak, it simply demonstrates wisdom and your obedience to God's Word!

CHAPTER 2

BROKENNESS TO PURPOSE

Our journeys were very similar prior to our union, we both were previously in marriages in which we knew God had not called us to. They were of our own doing, but nevertheless we spent years trying to bring life to dead situations in our own will, which of course ended in divorce. We utilized our time as single individuals to allow God to heal and develop us into the man and woman of God we are today.

Through the healing process we both learned that marital breakdown takes two individuals and we both understood that if we did not change as individuals we would repeat the same mistakes again and again, new faces, new names, but the same issues.

Our mistakes, pain and healing inevitably formed the ministry "Marriages of the Kingdom". We were divinely connected as husband and wife in 2011, my husband said he knew on our second date that I was his wife.

Through our union, our lifelong mission is to assist married couples and those seeking to be married to not make the same mistakes we did. Through our mistakes God has given us a platform to assist with building and developing marriages through Christian principles.

God showed me in a dream in 2010, our marriage ministry one year prior to meeting my husband. The marriage ministry was launched in April of 2012, while we served under our previous leader, Pastor George W. Dixon.

God confirmed that we were operating in our purpose, under the spirit and will of God when we spent our very first wedding anniversary counseling a couple for hours that were on the brink of separation that had been married 20+ years.

Our desire is to make ourselves available to any couple that says they want their marriage to reflect the Word of God and they are willing to "PUT IN THE WORK", it takes in order to have a happy, purpose-filled marriage!

We run across people constantly that tell us how our marriage inspires them and gives them hope for their own marriage or future marriage. We also encounter those that have openly said they are jealous of our marriage and that our acts of love towards each other actually irritates them. Our response is that you do not know the struggle we went through to get to this place, the beautifulness of our marriage was birthed through pain, trial and error! It simply requires you nurturing your relationship.

Marriage is work, if you are selfish in anyway please remain single, the pain we encountered was to birth a ministry that would bless others!

Our marriage is beautiful because we gave God full control of our lives and our marriage! Your marriage can and will flourish, if you totally submit to the Word of God and put the work in! Just know the closer you get to God, the closer you will get to your spouse.

Our Mistakes, Our Pain, Our Ministry!

Marriage Prayer

Please pray this over your marriage!

Dear God thank you so much for the blessing of marriage. Although we each have faults and disagree, please help us to continue to see the GOOD in each other. Help us to continue to LOVE each other unconditionally. PROTECT our marriage from outside threats. GUARD our hearts from temptation and the evil that tries to divide what you have joined together. We pray that our marriage grows and matures as we continue to enjoy our lives together according to your Word. Help us to be INTENTIONAL about showing love for each other. CONVICT our hearts when we are wrong and help us to be quick to forgive and restore any brokenness in our marriage. Bless our marriage and help us always to draw closer to You. In Jesus Name we pray, Amen!

CHAPTER 3

SPIRITUAL INTIMACY

What is intimacy? This means you allow your husband or wife to see you from the core, the inside out. We have to understand that intimacy is not just sex, you can have sex and not be intimate with your spouse. It takes time and you have to build trust first to truly know that your spouse will not mistreat you or use whatever you have shared with them as a means to hurt them later. If you can't "fight fair", you will definitely kill intimacy in your marriage.

If both husband and wife will seek to meet each other's needs and move from selfishness, they will create a friction that will produce a fire in their marriage, that no man or situation will be able to destroy. Adrian and I decided before we were married that we would put everything God had shown us into each other. We said to God and each other, if we were to marry again, we would do it the right way. Does this mean we get it "right" everyday? No, because we are human, but what keeps us on track, is the Word of God. If we can't find a common ground, we seek God's direction.

Usually when there is disconnect in the marriage, there is a lack of intimacy.

Spiritual intimacy is the foundation of every Christ-centered marriage and it sets the tone of your marriage and home. We are intentional about studying the Word of God and praying together consistently. These guidelines for our marriage help us so that we are able to continually grow together.

Our goal is to study the bible together weekly and pray together each night. Does this happen every night – no – but we stay as CONSISTENT as possible. We all have to be willing to invest in our relationship with each other and most importantly with God. We truly encourage this lifestyle for couples as this is the building block we utilize in marital counseling and it has been very effective and inspirational for many other couples.

There may be many reasons that spouses may not be able to pray and study together consistently, but if lack of intimacy and separation is an issue, it may be time for each of you to regain or begin to focus on the spiritual intimacy in your marriage. Spiritual intimacy sets the atmosphere for everything else in your marriage.

Worship invites the peace of God in church, so just think what it will do in your home, our first assignment and ministry begins within our marriage and home!

It is impossible to be in disagreement with each other, when you take the focus off yourselves and focus your attention on GOD! It is impossible to argue with each other when you are praying together!

There are some couples that feel their marriage is dead and they are just buying time and going through the motions day by day! Even though, your marriage has been broken for a very long time, God is saying if you want to heal and restore your marriage, HE can do it! He needs BOTH of you to give him the opportunity to PROVE His word to you, so that His glory can be revealed! DO NOT GIVE UP, just understand you are experiencing one of the seasons of marriage, winter does not last permanently!

CHAPTER 4

SEXUAL INTIMACY IN MARRIAGE

Through experience I have learned that my response to making love to my husband could have reminded me of bad past experiences had I not been healed prior to meeting him. As a teenager being molested, sex for many years appeared dirty to me. Many years prior to meeting my husband, I went through a healing process in which God restored me to the woman he created me to be and God renewed my thinking. Many women have been abused sexually, emotionally and physically, however the majority of them never share this due to shame, *even with their husbands.*

-My Testimony, Nicole

Husbands, do you know your wife's past? Husbands, I need you to know that it's not that your wife is rejecting you in the bedroom and that she does not love or want you, but understand if she has been abused in her past, it is very much possible that she looks at sex as "a bad experience". If sex has been presented to a woman prematurely and from a place of selfishness and deceit which occurs when molestation takes place, it can take away the pleasure and excitement which should transpire during lovemaking with her husband.

Wives, if you have been abused in any way whether emotionally, physically or sexually please seek help to heal. If you never heal you will never be able to allow your marriage to reach its fullest potential, please know your husband needs and wants all of you.

Sexual intimacy is what most people think of when they hear the word "intimate." Yes, intimacy can be love-making with your spouse, but is not limited to sexual activity. There is also non-sexual intimacy such as kissing, holding hands, back rubs and hugging. Men, please understand there are times when non-sexual intimacy may lead to sexual intimacy, however it should not every time, it takes a little more for women to get excited about the bedroom. This is one of the biggest complaints for some women, just know that sometimes your wife just wants to be held.

Married couples because our flesh is weak, the Word of God says to stop depriving one another, except by agreement for a time, so that you may devote yourselves to prayer, and come together again so that Satan will not tempt you because of your lack of self-control.

Wives, whatever you do, regardless of how upset you are, please do not deprive your husband of the one thing that brings joy to him more than anything else, out of anger. Sex was not created for purposes of bargaining or manipulation, God created it to bring pleasure and satisfaction to both the husband and wife.

Husbands, in order for you to get what it is you need, you have to be willing to do your part as well, help with the cooking, the cleaning, the children etc. Please make sure you help alleviate some of the daily stress your wife has, so she is in the mood and ready to make love to you. Men take time to find out what it is that excites your wife and get to it.

Husbands, the Holy Word says; As a loving hind and a graceful doe, Let her breasts - *your wife's breasts* satisfy you at all times; Be exhilarated always with her love.

Make your home a safe haven and peaceful place for each other, as well as the children. Yes, we have to address everyday life, but don't allow your home to be the place in which all the heaviness is downloaded. Here's a suggestion; if you have to discuss finances etc. change locations when the weather permits, go to the park with a picnic basket, sit down and enjoy each other at the same time! Some things have to be discussed, just change your approach! BE INTENTIONAL ABOUT YOUR MARRIAGE!

CHAPTER 5

AM I READY FOR MARRIAGE?

If you are single or divorced please answer these simple questions, to assist you with making a sound decision on whether or not you are ready for marriage. If you answer YES to either question please re-evaluate your decision to marry.

Men and women please understand, your wanting to be married and actually being prepared for marriage are two separate things!

The foundation of your relationship will determine its stability!

1. My fiancé does not have a relationship with Christ, but once we are married that will automatically change?

2. The time you spend alone with just yourself is boring?

3. If you were in a previous relationship, do you still blame that person for the relationship ending?

4. Does the person you are dating currently remind you of someone you dated or was married to previously?

5. I am still grieving my previous relationship; I am in the process of healing?

6. I believe that once I get married, I will truly be happy?

7. There are some things that I am unwilling to change; my future spouse will have to accept me as is, because this is who I am?

8. I am unsure of my purpose in life, but my spouse will help me to decide?

9. Once I get married I feel it is important that we keep our finances separate just in case, this person is wrong for me?

10. Once we are married my spouse should not have any other friends other than myself?

Apologizing doesn't always mean that you're wrong and your spouse is right. It means you value your marriage more than your ego!

We all have a great opportunity to strengthen or weaken our marriage and spouse every time we speak. If we learn the art of CONTROLLING OUR TONGUE, our marriages will be so much better and stronger!

30 DAY GUIDE

Reflection,

Inspiration &

Application

Day 1

Reflection:

Marriage is not selfish, it is about sacrifice and obedience; marriage will cost you; your heart, your time, your comfort and your pride. The couples who learn to die to themselves are the ones who will experience the power and fulfillment that comes with a meaningful, happy and purpose-filled marriage! If you can kill your flesh, the power of God can resurrect your marriage!

Inspiration:

Always be humble and gentle. Be patient with each other, making allowance for each other's faults because of your love. Make every effort to keep yourselves united in the Spirit, binding yourselves together with peace. - Ephesians 4:2-3

Application:

Couples take the time today to do something your spouse loves, that may or may not be something that is necessarily of enjoyment to you.

_____

_____

_____

_____

_____

_____

_____

Day 2

Reflection:

In marriage you will always have disagreements and conflict, the disagreement is never the issue, the way you communicate your dissatisfaction is what will determine the outcome.

Inspiration:

A gentle answer deflects anger, but harsh words make tempers flare. -Proverbs 15:1.

Application:

Sit down with your spouse and set standards and rules in place of the do's and don'ts of your marriage disagreements.

_____

_____

_____

_____

_____

_____

_____

_____

_____

Day 3

Reflection:

An emotionally stable person can love, serve and give to their spouse, even when their spouse is not reciprocating these actions. Emotionally stable people will never go tick for tack.

Inspiration:

So I say, let the Holy Spirit guide your lives. Then you won't be doing what your sinful nature craves. - Galatians 5:16

Application:

Daily you will refrain from having the mindset that "I will only do for you" based upon how you treat me.

_____

_____

_____

_____

_____

_____

_____

_____

_____

_____

Day 4

Reflection:

You must always surround yourself with friends and family who respect and will strengthen your marriage and remove yourself from people who may entice you to compromise your character or create separation between yourself and your spouse.

Inspiration:

Don't be fooled by those who say such things, for "bad company corrupts good character." -1 Corinthians 15:33

Application:

Take an evaluation of the people closest to you and your spouse to see if their presence produces life or death to your marriage.

Day 5

Reflection:

Never lie to your spouse. Lies break trust which is the foundation of every marriage. You cannot have a healthy and lasting marriage lying to each other. The truth should always be your only option.

Inspiration:

The Lord detests lying lips, but he delights in those who tell the truth. -Proverbs 12:22

Application:

Always practice honesty even if the outcome is not favorable for you.

_____

_____

_____

_____

_____

_____

_____

_____

_____

_____

Day 6

Reflection:

There will be days in which you will not like your spouse because they will make mistakes and do things that may hurt you. Don't forget that God continues to love and cover us even when we don't quite deserve it!

Inspiration:

Instead, be kind to each other, tenderhearted, forgiving one another, just as God through Christ has forgiven you.
-Ephesians 4:32

Application:

Make a decision today that you will not continue to hold your spouse hostage to their past mistakes.

_____

_____

_____

_____

_____

_____

_____

_____

Day 7

Reflection:
Every husband and wife has the power to uplift their spouse or tear them down. You have the power to build a king or queen through the words you speak to your spouse, which in turn will either build or tear down your marriage.

Inspiration:
Don't use foul or abusive language. Let everything you say be good and helpful, so that your words will be an encouragement to those who hear them. -Ephesians 4:29

Application:
Decide today what you will do with the power God has given you to speak into the life of your spouse. Exercise your power by only speaking positivity regarding your spouse.

_____

_____

_____

_____

_____

_____

_____

_____

_____

Day 8

Reflection:

Couples please pray and study the scriptures together, your marriage will only gain strength if it is controlled by the Voice and the Word of God.

Inspiration:

Oh, the joys of those who do not follow the advice of the wicked, or stand around with sinners, or join in with mockers. But they delight in the law of the Lord, meditating on it day and night. They are like trees planted along the riverbank, bearing fruit each season. Their leaves never wither, and they prosper in all they do.
-Psalm 1:1-3

Application:

Put together a daily prayer routine and weekly study routine with your spouse to develop spiritual intimacy in your marriage.

Day 9

Reflection:

Let go of your past hurts and pain, so that your marriage can flourish as God intended, move forward. No longer allow people and situations to destroy your future and the happiness in your marriage.

Inspiration:

But forget all that - it is nothing compared to what I am going to do. For I am about to do something new. See, I have already begun! Do you not see it? I will make a pathway through the wilderness. I will create rivers in the dry wasteland. -Isaiah 43:18-19

Application:

Write down any past hurts or pain you still have and make a decision through prayer that you will no longer allow those things to prevent you from having abundance in your marriage.

_____

_____

_____

_____

_____

_____

_____

Day 10

Reflection:

Every spouse has an opinion, if at any time making a decision conflicts, we should always refer back to the Word of God, which is not opinion but truth.

Inspiration:

Then Elijah stood in front of them and said, "How much longer will you waver, hobbling between two opinions? If the Lord is God, follow him!" -1 Kings 18:21

Application:

Make it a routine to pray before making decisions that will have an impact on your marriage and family.

_____

_____

_____

_____

_____

_____

_____

_____

_____

Day 11

Reflection:

Nagging destroys marriages, because someone is going to shut down eventually, if you are not communicating properly the marriage begins to die slowly, lack of communication is one of the major reasons for divorce.

Inspiration:

It's better to live alone in the corner of an attic than with a quarrelsome wife in a lovely home. -Proverbs 21:19

Application:

Make the most of each day, focus on the things your spouse is great at and intentionally make a decision to overlook the things you feel they should or should not be doing.

_____

_____

_____

_____

_____

_____

_____

_____

_____

Day 12

Reflection:

Couples we have a choice, either have a happy and peaceful marriage or have the last word.

Inspiration:

The one who has knowledge uses words with restraint, and whoever has understanding is even tempered. Even fools are thought wise if they keep silent, and discerning if they hold their tongues. -Prov. 17:27-28

Application:

Even if you feel you are right, it's best to be quiet at times!

_____

_____

_____

_____

_____

_____

_____

_____

_____

_____

Day 13

Reflection:

Husbands learn to romance your wife throughout the day, remember that romance for a woman is not sex, she needs non-sexual attention in order to be excited and ready for the sexual attention that you need.

Wives do not use sex as a weapon or bargaining tool against your husband.

Inspiration:

Do not deprive one another except with consent for a time, that you may give yourselves to fasting and prayer; and come together again so that Satan does not tempt you because of your lack of self-control.-1 Cor. 7:5

Application:

Husbands identify your wife's love language and needs, serve her because you simply want to please her.

Wives try to initiate sex with your husbands, they will greatly appreciate it.

_____

_____

_____

_____

_____

Day 14

Reflection:

Please pray for each other and with each other! Prayer is one of the most powerful and meaningful things we can do for our marriage. Praying together produces a deeper intimacy in your marriage. I know that if you've never done this in your marriage it can be awkward. Because you are bearing your soul and confessing your sins during prayer to God in front of your spouse, which puts you in a very vulnerable place with your spouse. Your marriage is composed of (3) - God, you and your spouse and this is where you should be comfortable enough to release everything in you, your spouse is not there to judge you but to cover and build you. It may be uncomfortable at first, but trust us, it is VERY powerful.

Inspiration:

Devote yourselves to prayer with an alert mind and a thankful heart. -Colossians 4:2

Application:

Please be intentional about praying at least once a day with your spouse.

_____

_____

_____

_____

Day 15

Reflection:
Encourage your spouse, nothing can replace the encouragement or words of appreciation that your spouse hears from you. We should encourage our spouse many more times than we correct or disapprove of things they do or not do. Let's work on increasing how often we tell our spouse how much we appreciate them. Speaking life to each other is necessary to have a marriage that resembles the love of Jesus!

Inspiration:
I have not stopped thanking God for you. I pray for you constantly... -Ephesians 1:16

Application:
Today is a day of encouragement; tell your spouse what it is you truly appreciate about them.

_____

_____

_____

_____

_____

_____

_____

Day 16

Reflection:

In marriage you are in the same boat so if it sinks, you both drown. Blaming and pointing fingers will not build your marriage.

Inspiration:

Make every effort to keep yourselves united in the Spirit, binding yourselves together with peace. -Ephesians 4:3

Application:

Couples must have the mindset that we are in this together regardless of what happens, your spouse's mistake is also your mistake.

_____

_____

_____

_____

_____

_____

_____

_____

_____

Day 17

Reflection:

In order for your marriage to succeed, you have to be "TEACHABLE". If you think no one can give you direction and speak into your life especially your spouse, your marriage is bound to fail!

Inspiration:

In the same way, you who are younger must accept the authority of the elders. And all of you, dress yourselves in humility as you relate to one another, for "God opposes the proud but gives grace to the humble." -1 Peter 5:5

Application:

You must have an open mind and open line of communication with your spouse you cannot take constructive criticism personally.

_____

_____

_____

_____

_____

_____

_____

_____

Day 18

Reflection:

There is no perfect marriage, because we are not perfect spouses!

Inspiration:

And now, dear brothers and sisters, one final thing. Fix your thoughts on what is true, and honorable, and right, and pure, and lovely, and admirable. Think about things that are excellent and worthy of praise. - Philippians 4:8

Application:

If you stop focusing on what *YOU THINK* is wrong with your spouse, you will find happiness and peace within yourself and your marriage.

_____

_____

_____

_____

_____

_____

_____

_____

Day 19

Reflection:

Your role in marriage is not to change your spouse but to love them!

Inspiration:

This is my commandment: Love each other in the same way I have loved you. -John 15:12

Application:

Tell your spouse on today, I love you for who you are and as you are!

_____

_____

_____

_____

_____

_____

_____

_____

_____

_____

_____

Day 20

Reflection:

Be a safe place for each other to come home and share things with. Confide in each other, have fun with each other, help each other – be your spouse's #1 fan.

Inspiration:

Two people are better off than one, for they can help each other succeed. If one person falls, the other can reach out and help. But someone who falls alone is in real trouble. -Ecclesiastes 4:9-10

Application:

What will you do today to make your home a place of peace?

_____

_____

_____

_____

_____

_____

_____

_____

_____

_____

Day 21

Reflection:

The only time you should compete with your spouse is if you are trying to "out love" them.

Inspiration:

For even the Son of Man came not to be served but to serve others and to give his life as a ransom for many. -Mark 10:45

Application:

Ask your spouse each day, what can I do to make your life better?

_____

_____

_____

_____

_____

_____

_____

_____

_____

_____

_____

Day 22

Reflection:

Marriage means, I STILL LOVE YOU and I WILL STILL MEET YOUR NEEDS, EVEN IF I'M ANGRY AT YOU! God's spirit will always direct you to do the right thing!

Inspiration:

Most important of all, continue to show deep love for each other, for love covers a multitude of sins. -1 Peter 4:8

Application:

If you have had a disagreement, fight through your emotions and do something you know your spouse would really appreciate.

_____

_____

_____

_____

_____

_____

_____

_____

_____

_____

Day 23

Reflection:

Get your priorities right! God is your first priority and should be the source of your life, not your spouse. Your spouse was never meant to provide all of your emotional and spiritual needs. Each of us needs to spend time alone with God every day. Your second priority is your spouse. Children, ministry, business, family or careers should never take priority over your spouse.

Inspiration:

And you must love the Lord your God with all your heart, all your soul, and all your strength. -Deuteronomy 6:5

For husbands, this means love your wives, just as Christ loved the church. He gave up his life for her. -Ephesians 5:25

For wives, this means submit to your husbands as to the Lord. -Ephesians 5:22

Application:

Take a deep look with your spouse at the areas that need to change, so your priorities are ordered God's way.

_____

_____

_____

_____

_____

Day 24

Reflection:

We have to serve each other without expectations! Marriage isn't always going to be equal. Remember that Christ loves us unconditionally and that is how we are called to love.

Inspiration:

Love is patient and kind. Love is not jealous or boastful or proud or rude. It does not demand its own way. It is not irritable, and it keeps no record of being wronged. 1 Corinthians 13:4-5

Application:

Show a love gesture to your spouse without expecting anything in return.

_____

_____

_____

_____

_____

_____

_____

_____

_____

Day 25

Reflection:

Our marriages are like flowers, if we water and provide nourishment to them they will grow, if we neglect them they will wither away!

Inspiration:

It's not important who does the planting, or who does the watering. What's important is that God makes the seed grow. The one who plants and the one who waters work together with the same purpose. And both will be rewarded for their own hard work. For we are both God's workers. And you are God's field. You are God's building.
-1 Corinthians 3:7-9

Application:

Make sure you have constant and uninterrupted time with your spouse spiritually, emotionally and physically.

_____

_____

_____

_____

_____

_____

_____

Day 26

Reflection:

Never put expectations on your spouse that they can never meet, it sets them up for failure and sets you up for disappointment! Worship God not each other.

Inspiration:

Let all that I am wait quietly before God, for my hope is in him.
-Psalm 62:5

Application:

Give your spouse room to make mistakes, remember you are growing and maturing together daily.

_____

_____

_____

_____

_____

_____

_____

_____

_____

_____

Day 27

Reflection:

Remember that your spouse is not your enemy. Your spouse is your biggest earthly gift from God, you must work your differences out together.

Inspiration:

A kingdom divided by civil war will collapse. Similarly, a family splintered by feuding will fall apart. -Mark 3:24-25

Application:

Understand if your spouse disagrees with you, it does not mean they are against you, it simply means you do not think alike regarding every situation.

_____

_____

_____

_____

_____

_____

_____

_____

_____

Day 28

Reflection:

As individuals we ALL have to go to GOD and say clean ME up, not my spouse! If I'm better, my marriage will be better! Refrain from pointing fingers and look within!

Inspiration:

Create in me a clean heart, O God. Renew a loyal spirit within me.
-Psalm 51:10

Application:

Today I will seek God to assist me with making myself better, because change begins within me.

Day 29

Reflection:

Are you dating your spouse? If not, your marriage is withering away slowly. Make time for you and your spouse *ONLY*. It is not an option, it's a *MUST*!

Inspiration

Let us think of ways to motivate one another to acts of love and good works. And let us not neglect our meeting together, as some people do, but encourage one another, especially now that the day of his return is drawing near. -Hebrews 10:24-25

Application:

Schedule consistent date nights with your spouse when possible, remember dating does not necessarily mean spending money. Dating is the time you spend with your spouse to give them your undivided attention, the location is irrelevant.

_____

_____

_____

_____

_____

_____

_____

_____

Day 30

Reflection:

Ministry starts at HOME, not CHURCH! There are times we are not even on speaking terms with our spouses, but we are in church shouting, prophesying, speaking in tongues, preaching, playing instruments and teaching! Sorry, but God does not and will not accept this.

Inspiration:

Sensible people control their temper; they earn respect by overlooking wrongs. -Proverbs 19:11

Application:

I will make sure that I understand my first priority is to be in right relationship with God, then my spouse; if I fall short I will seek God for guidance in my marriage.

_____

_____

_____

_____

_____

_____

_____

_____

Begin to make positive declarations over your marriage daily! There is power in your tongue! Your marriage will reflect what you speak about it.

Say this with your spouse, Our marriage reflects the love of Jesus, we walk in agreement and there is no division among us!

www.ingramcontent.com/pod-product-compliance
Lightning Source LLC
Chambersburg PA
CBHW060158070426
42447CB00033B/2204